Rookie choices®

D0406463

THE SIDEWALK PATROL

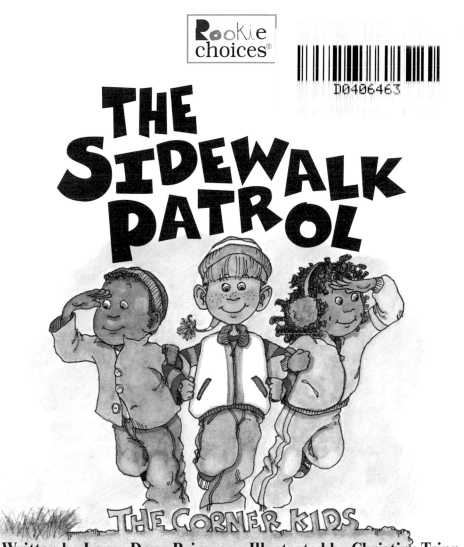

THE CORNER KIDS

Written by Larry Dane Brimner • Illustrated by Christine Tripp

Children's Press®
A Division of Scholastic Inc.
New York • Toronto • London • Auckland • Sydney
Mexico City • New Delhi • Hong Kong
Danbury, Connecticut

For Anne P. Anderson, Teacher of all Years
—L.D.B.

For my grandson, Kobe
—C.T.

Reading Consultants
Linda Cornwell
Literacy Specialist

Katharine A. Kane
Education Consultant
(Retired, San Diego County Office of Education and San Diego State University)

Library of Congress Cataloging-in-Publication Data
Brimner, Larry Dane
    The Sidewalk patrol / written by Larry Dane Brimner ; illustrated by Christine Tripp.
        p. cm. —(Rookie choices)
    Summary: Gabby and her friends take time to move some bicycles so that their blind
neighbor can walk on the sidewalk.
    ISBN: 0-516-22537-5 (lib. bdg.)   0-516-27387-6 (pbk.)
    [1. Thoughtfulness—Fiction. 2. Kindness—Fiction. 3. Blind—Fiction. 4. Physically
handicapped—Fiction.] I. Tripp, Christine, ill. II. Title. III. Series.

PZ7. B767 Si 2002
[E]—dc21

                                                              2001003865

This book is about
respect for others.

The Corner Kids raced down the sidewalk toward the bus stop.

Alex, Gabby, and Three J called themselves the Corner Kids. Gabby and Alex lived in an apartment building on one corner. Three J's apartment was on the other corner. They were best friends.

"We better hurry," Alex said.

"If we miss the bus," said Gabby, "we won't get to go ice-skating until next weekend."

"Road block!" Alex called over his shoulder to Gabby and Three J.

A bunch of bicycles blocked the sidewalk. Some big kids stood nearby. They were talking to each other and laughing.

9

Alex stopped running.
So did Gabby and Three J.

"Road hogs," Alex mumbled.
Carefully, he stepped around
the bicycles. He turned to wait for
Gabby and Three J. That's when
he saw Ms. Michaels.

11

Ms. Michaels lived in Three J's apartment building. She and her dog, Elaine, walked every afternoon.

"We're out for our exercise," Ms. Michaels liked to say.

ROUTES
99 101
34 92
81

"The bus!" Gabby said, pointing.
She started for the bus stop.

"Wait!" Alex called. He watched Ms. Michaels and Elaine. "We need to move these bikes. Elaine won't let Ms. Michaels walk in the street."

"But we'll miss the bus," said Gabby.

"Alex is right," said Three J,
moving a bicycle.

19

Gabby nodded. "We can skate next weekend," she said, and she pitched in to help.

"Hey, those are our bikes!" hollered one of the big kids.

"They're in the way," Alex said. He rolled another bicycle to the edge of the sidewalk.

The big kid shrugged.

Just then, Ms. Michaels and Elaine walked up. Elaine wagged her tail.

"It's all clear, Ms. Michaels,"
Three J said.

"We moved some bikes so you and
Elaine could get by," explained Alex.

"Thank you," said Ms. Michaels. Then she laughed. "I guess this means you're my official sidewalk patrol."

The Corner Kids thought that was cool, and so did Elaine.

ABOUT THE AUTHOR

Larry Dane Brimner studied literature and writing at San Diego State University and taught school for twenty years. The author of more than seventy-five books for children, many of them Children's Press titles, he enjoys meeting young readers and writers when he isn't at his computer.

ABOUT THE ILLUSTRATOR

Christine Tripp lives in Ottawa, Canada, with her husband Don; four grown children—Elizabeth, Erin, Emily, and Eric; son-in-law Jason; grandsons Brandon and Kobe; four cats; and one very large, scruffy puppy named Jake.